THE COMPLETE ISLE OF WIGHT COASTAL FOOTPATH

70 MILES ON A SCENIC, COASTAL WALK OF THE ISLAND, DIVIDED INTO 5 SECTIONS FOR DAY WALKS OR 1 COMPLETE CIRCUIT

Experience the Downs, Cliffs and Coastline of this Magnificent Island

AN
ESSENTIAL GUIDE TO
HELP YOU COMPLETE
THE
ISLE OF WIGHT COASTAL FOOTPATH

BRIAN SMAILES

Other books by the same author

THE YORKSHIRE DALES TOP TEN
ISBN 0-9526900-5-5

THE LAKELAND TOP TEN
ISBN 0-9526900-3-9

THE DERBYSHIRE TOP TEN
ISBN 1-903568-03-X

THE SCOTTISH COAST TO COAST WALK
ISBN 0-9526900-8-X

17 WALKS IN GLEN NEVIS
ISBN 1-903568-05-6

ISLE OF WIGHT, NORTH TO SOUTH-EAST TO WEST
ISBN 1-903568-07-2

JOHN O'GROATS TO LANDS END
ISBN 0-9526900-4-7

THE NATIONAL 3 PEAKS WALK
ISBN 0-9526900-7-1

THE NOVICES GUIDE TO THE LYKE WAKE WALK
ISBN 0-9526900-1-2

THE YORKSHIRE 3 PEAKS WALK
ISBN 1-903568-01-3

THE 1066 COUNTRY WALK
ISBN 1-903568-00-5

MILLENNIUM CYCLE RIDES IN 1066 COUNTRY (EAST SUSSEX)
ISBN 1-903568-04-8

ISBN 0-9526900-6-3
FIRST PUBLISHED 2000

SECOND EDITION 2002
CHALLENGE PUBLICATIONS
7, EARLSMERE DRIVE, BARNSLEY. S71 5HH
www.chall-pub.fsnet.co.uk
E mail challengepublications@yahoo.co.uk

THE AUTHOR

Brian Smailes

Holds the record for the fastest 4 and 5 continuous crossings of the Lyke Wake Walk over the North York Moors. He completed the 210 miles over rough terrain on 5 crossings in June 1995 taking 85 hours and 50 minutes.

Brian lectures on outdoor pursuit courses and between these travels extensively on walking expeditions and projects around Great Britain.

Long distance running and canoeing are other sports he enjoys, completing 25 marathons and canoeing the Caledonian Canal 3 times.

His most recent venture involved cycling from Lands End to John O`Groats in August 2001, a journey of over 900 miles in 6 days 13 hours 18 minutes. This involved carrying food, clothing and tent, and was completed without support between both ends.

CONTENTS

PLATES

INTRODUCTION

The Isle of Wight coastal footpath is a total of 70 miles of paths, roads and tracks. The route is described in 5 daily walks which, when joined together completes the coastal footpath.

Most of the route is well defined and signposted, however there are some sections, which are not. Certain sections of the route, particularly along the cliffs on the south of the island, are prone to erosion. Extra care needs to be taken on these sections and walkers should keep away from the edge of the cliffs at all times. There may be diversions from time to time on this section of the route.

There are some outstanding areas of scenery, particularly over the Downs leading to the Needles, Alum Bay, Cowes front and Culver Down. Once you have experienced this walk it will never be forgotten.

Because the Isle of Wight is small, you may find it easier to walk one section at a time, using local transport to take you to and from a central base. I recommend checking the bus times for each individual section before you leave.

Those walkers who are familiar with backpacking will equally enjoy walking the full route over a number of days. To assist with this all the campsites on route are included to enable you to plan and book ahead and all are of a high standard.

Refreshments have not been overlooked and a list of the public houses you pass, where you should be able to obtain bar meals and a wide selection of drinks, are included.

Wherever you are on the coastal footpath you are not far away from habitation. Compass bearings are unnecessary, as the detailed description of the route is safe enough, providing you keep away from cliff edges and walk sensibly on the roads.

Read on to experience the sheer delights of this walk, as I did. To complement this guide I recommend the Ordnance Survey No.29 Outdoor Leisure Map of the Isle of Wight, which should be used in conjunction with this book.

All Coastal Footpath Signs will be referred to as C.FP. usually followed by a number. All Public Footpath signs will be referred to as P.F. sometimes followed by a number.

THE ISLE OF WIGHT

This island may be relatively small, measuring approximately 23miles by 13miles, at the widest points but it holds a wealth of treasures. There are Castles, Stately Homes, Manor Houses, Abbeys and Churches as well as the excellent scenery over Tennyson Down, St. Catherine's Point and Bembridge Down, to name but a few. Over 500 miles of footpaths and bridleways cover the island, enabling walkers to experience the delights of the varied landscape.

The island was once part of the mainland, about 6000B.C. but the sea gradually encroached on the area as the ice sheets melted, producing the island we see today. Stone Age man were inhabitants here, also Bronze Age man with their barrows and ditches, and more recent visitors, the Romans who left villas in Newport and Morton.

Christianity came to the island in the 7th century, and a few hundred years later the influence of William the Conqueror brought about the building of Carisbrooke Castle. The crown has owned the island since 1293. Queen Victoria built Osborne House here in 1845 as her holiday retreat.

Alfred, Lord Tennyson had a home here and a cross is erected on Tennyson Down near the Needles to mark his life and achievement as the Poet Laureate.

Newport is the principal and most central town on the island, with a number of resorts and villages situated around the coastline. Inland there are a number of small villages and a network of roads giving access to all parts. Being an island many of the population have boats and enjoy work and leisure pursuits connected with the sea.

Yarmouth harbour is a fine example of the sea faring tradition as a busy harbour for pleasure boats throughout the summer months.

There are many attractions here for visitors and those you pass on this coastal path walk are mentioned in this book, should you wish to visit them. You will undoubtedly find the local people are friendly, helpful and welcoming to everyone.

ACCESS TO THE ISLAND

Portsmouth to Ryde
Wightlink: Fast Cat/Ferry	0870 5827744
Hovercraft	01983 811000
High Speed Catamaran	0870 5827744

Portsmouth to Fishbourne
Wightlink Ferry	0870 5827744

Southampton to Cowes
Red Funnel Ferry	023 80334010

Lymington to Yarmouth
Wightlink Ferry	0870 5827744

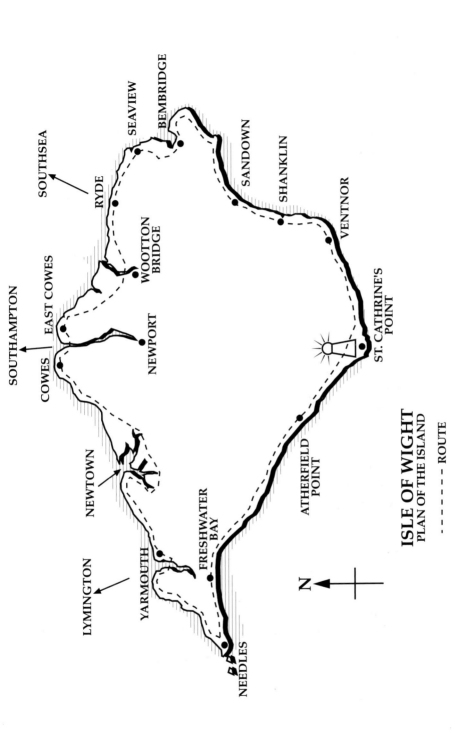

ISLE OF WIGHT
PLAN OF THE ISLAND

- - - - ROUTE

N

EQUIPMENT

Remember when walking along the cliff tops it can be extremely windy and exposed. To enable you to enjoy this walk, I recommend the following clothing/equipment items. Depending whether you are on day walks or walking the full route you may need to add or delete some items on this check-list: -

1. Waterproof/Windproof Jacket
2. Small Tent/Sleeping Bag
3. Cooking Stove/Fuel/Matches
4. Pans/Cutlery/Plate/Cup/Food/Water Bottle
5. Sunscreen/Insect Repellent
6. Boots and Trainers/spare socks
7. Rucksack/Day Sack
8. Gloves/Hat
9. Suitable Trousers (not jeans)
10. First Aid Kit/Whistle/Survival Bag
11. Torch/Spare Bulb/Batteries
12. Map/Compass
13. Spare Clothing

Most importantly do not walk in high heels and/or jeans and T-shirt because you will quickly get aching or blistered feet and no doubt feel cold. Jeans can chafe the skin and take a long time to dry if wet as well as drawing the body heat.

Prepare your equipment carefully and you will feel the benefit when walking or camping.

SECTION 1
Ryde Pier to Hope Beach, Shanklin
Time to Allow 7 hrs
Total Distance 14.1 miles
Start G.R. 594929

Leaving Ryde Pier terminal, which was built in 1824, turn left and walk along the esplanade passing the bowling alley and small harbour. Continue past the boating lake keeping left along the promenade and passing Appley Tower to the right walking towards Puckpool Point. Keep on the middle path as you walk around the point. You come to a toll road (no charge) where you should see Nettlestone Point ahead, with Horse Sand Fort and No Man's Land Fort, built around 1870, out to sea. A sign near to Nettlestone Point states C.FP. R91 along the edge of the sea wall.

Seaview Yacht Club is on your left as the path winds around, still keeping to the sea wall. Follow the road round to your right then up into the village passing the Seaview Hotel halfway up the road. Turn left at Pier Road mini roundabout. A sign points to Seagrove Bay. The metalled road turns to gravel for a short distance as you walk behind some houses on a narrow tree lined lane to Seagrove Bay slipway.

At Seagrove slipway a sign beside the toilets states C.FP. R74. Turn right and walk uphill before bearing left up a narrow private leafy lane. An opening at the side of a gate is for walkers only at the start of the lane. Walk for 700m passing the Priory Hotel on your left then bear left towards St. Helens. This is a narrow lane with houses to the left and open fields to the right.

You emerge onto a metalled road with a sign C.FP. and Bembridge 2miles. Turn right and descend towards Bembridge. Pass through double gates then turn right for 100m to a sign C.FP. R85. Go through the kissing gate, across a field and through a small wood, then over a stile. Walk along the side of a field to a stile emerging onto a metalled road following the C.FP. sign. *(Should you intend camping here you can enter the nearby campsite on your left)*. Cross the road and walk over the Duver. This was once the old golf links but is now owned by the National Trust. Branch off to your right on a path near the car park, which takes you along a causeway spanning the tidal area. This was the old St. Helens Mill Dam wall and you should walk over its sluice bridges with care.

Pass some houses, then at the marina bear left over the footbridge crossing the river Yar. Emerge onto Embankment Road, which is a causeway built in 1878 and keep left passing the yacht club on your left. Walk for 1600m to the sharp bend just before Bembridge Village. Turn left opposite the Pilot Boat Inn where a sign points to the C.FP. Take the left hand pebbled road, which becomes a narrow leafy lane behind the houses. On a stony path turn left and descend to another sign saying C.FP. which is to the right. Go down a narrow lane by Colonels Hard to the beach and walk for 300m on the beach to some stone steps ascending along side a wooden fence. Turn left and the lifeboat station is 100m ahead. A C.FP. sign points left on a narrow path at the edge of the beach emerging at the lifeboat station. Walk along the beach for a short distance to a sign C.FP. turning right up some stone steps then walking up a path along the right side of Bembridge Hotel and leisure club. Turn left then right into a housing estate. Take the second left along Beachfield Road at another sign. This path takes you to the sea again by the Crab & Lobster pub.

Pass the front of the pub and along a narrow path at the top of the cliff. Follow the C.FP. sign and in your direction of travel you will see the cliffs around Culver Down and in the distance a monument on the hill. This is your next destination.

Follow the cliff top path passing Bembridge school playing fields and through a small wood. You arrive near the white cliffs with a caravan site nearby. Take the right path by the side of Sandhills Caravan Park and pass some chalets before ascending a steep chalk path up the hill to the monument on Culver Down summit. This was erected to the memory of the Earl of Yarborough in 1849. Culver Down is a chalk headland and the cliffs around it a bird sanctuary. The summit is 99m above sea level with impressive views of the island and coastline and is a good picnic stop.

Go through the metal gate near the monument, turn right, pass the coastguard kiosk near the cottages then bear left following the sign descending the Down towards Sandown (Plate 1). Do not go along the metalled road. It is an enjoyable walk into Sandown, emerging at the car park at Yaverland with the beach and groynes to your left and Sandown Zoo a little further on to your right. Sandown is the islands largest resort.

Walk along the promenade, through the main street of Sandown with shops on both sides of the road. Just past the shops is a signpost to Whitewater. Turn left and descend a short road back to the promenade. Carry on towards Shanklin passing the beach huts and kiosks (Plate 2), arriving at Hope Beach.

Should you be returning to Ryde or camping at Shanklin, then at the bend in the road at Hope Beach turn right and ascend to Shanklin centre to the campsite or connect with a bus to take you back to your starting point.

SECTION 2
Hope Beach, Shanklin to Atherfield (Chine Farm Campsite)
Time to Allow 8½ hrs
Total Distance 13.3 miles
Start G.R. 587818

Starting at Hope Beach walk south along the promenade, past the small arcades and shops towards the cliffs near Luccombe Village. Pass the small clock tower on the sea front to a roundabout and a metalled road to your right. A small sign points to Appley Steps and Luccombe along by the beach and pub. Continue past the Fishermans Cottage pub to Appley Steps just beyond. Ascend the steep cliffs to Rylstone Gardens, which has a tearoom at the side. There are good views looking back towards Culver Down from here.

Continue up this road then bear left and ascend Luccombe Road passing Luccombe Hall Country House Hotel on your left. The C.FP. continues on a narrow path following the sign at the end of the road towards Luccombe tea gardens. Further on another sign states the same; keep to the left road here by the turning circle signed C.FP. SS2.

Walk through the tea gardens staying on the well marked undulating path. You see 5 other signs but follow C.FP. SS2 sign, walking on a gravel path between thatched houses.

You come to an area known as Bonchurch Land Slip (this is taken from the original land slip of 1810) on route to Bonchurch. The path passes through a wood and a kissing gate. Follow it around and up some steps before seeing 3 green signs, one states Bonchurch and Ventnor to the left. Take this route following the undulating narrow path through the wood. Your path then bears off right towards Bonchurch and Ventnor; there is a handrail up some steps here.

The original path that went straight on is overgrown and dangerous, so it is advisable to take the short detour up to the right, rejoining the original path further on. Continue on past a sign P.F. V58B ascending a mud and rutted track and finally emerging onto a wider track beside some houses. Pass the car park beside Monks Bay Cottage. The path forks, take the right path where you will pass a seat and a plaque depicting Monks Bay/Bonchurch revetment.

A sign states C.FP. V69 Ventnor 1¼ miles. Cross a waterfall descending into Horseshoe Bay onto a metalled road then to a gravel car park. Follow the path along at the base of white cliffs near the sea on a recently restored section, passing in front of some holiday chalets. Stay on the promenade all the way around.

You come to a car park on the promenade where there is a waterfall on your right and a children's paddling pool. Continue past the Mill Bay pub on the front and a small clock monument.

Continue along the front, passing the kiosks until you reach the Spy Glass Inn. Turn right up a metalled road to La Falaise car park, which you go through onto the grass at the far side where a path takes you towards St. Catherine's Point. A tarmac path leads along the cliff side. Follow the signs for C.FP. V85 and Botanic Gardens where a concrete path winds around the headland down to Castle Cove. Walk around Castle Cove past some houses to a kiosk where you turn onto a steeply rising path. A sign states C.FP. left and up a flight of steps to your right. At the top turn left passing a cricket pitch on the right.

Plate 1
Descending from Culver Down towards Sandown.

Plate 2
Walking along the sea front at Shanklin.

A stile and sign on your right leads to the Botanical Gardens, do not go this way, but follow the sign C.FP. V90, which is near another stile, a kissing gate, and some steps off to the left. Take the 6 steps up to your left then down the flight of steps on the other side to a narrow field with a sign saying C.FP. Ascend the field to the right corner, then descend the next field, which has a children's play area on the right.

Where the signpost is pointing to Orchard House, turn right there, along a short path by the side of the rare breeds park to the main A3055 road between Ventnor and Niton. Turn left, walking along the road (Undercliff Drive) with care past the front of the rare breeds park until you come to Seven Sisters Road. A sign points to the village hall.

Turn right and ascend the winding road, steeply in places, with a sharp right hand bend up to the top of the cliff. Look for a P.F. sign V74 on your left at the top. Go up some steps and over a stile onto a short grass path, which you stay on for 3.3km to Niton.

There are excellent views looking out to sea and across the land as you walk on this cliff top path. Two radio masts and buildings are nearby the path as you walk on this high level path.

Follow the distinct path as you approach Niton, onto a gravel track turning right for a short distance to a blue C.FP. sign. This leads to the main road through Niton. Turn right, cross the road, then immediately left. A sign states C.FP. NT32 and Blackgang where the gravel track initially bears right and ascends following a sign to Blackgang via cliff tops. The hill slightly off to your right is St. Catherine's Hill 237m and has a T.V. transmitter and a 'trig' point on the summit. Go over the stile and along the side of the field, then over another stile.

Continue along the cliff top (Plate 3) to a car park just past the look out point. Climb over the stile and walk down a narrow path to Blackgang Chine. Cross another stile into a grass field following the hedge to another stile leading onto the road. By crossing the field it avoids walking on the road for a short distance.

Walk down the right side of the road and after going around a right hand bend follow the sign Public Bridleway-Chale Church C15 to your left. Turn right at the end of the tree lined path. Your route to the Needles is visible in the distance ahead. Follow the metalled road down to the main A3055 road near Chale Church.

Turn left passing the church and telephone box and continue to just past Cliff Farm. Turn left opposite the entrance to the Wight Mouse Inn, going over a stile. This takes you over a short footbridge and back onto the cliff top. Proceed around the cliff top path, which may be overgrown in parts, keeping away from the edge. Look for a sign C.FP. C18 pointing back to the road. On reaching the road turn left walking for 300m to Whale Chine car park. Turn down the side of the car park back to the cliff top path following the sign C.FP. SW30.

Follow the cliff path passing a row of cottages and a holiday park on your right. Just before a campsite is Shepherds Chine where you need to walk slightly inland. Look for a small yellow arrow taking you down a path and up the other side of the chine. Follow the track into the campsite if you are camping at the end of this section; alternatively go to the road to catch a bus back to your original start point.

Plate 3
Checking the map on the cliff top path above St. Catherine's Point.

Plate 4

The cliff top path above Brightstone Bay with Tennyson Down, top left.

SECTION 3
Atherfield (Chine Farm Campsite) to Colwell Bay
Time to Allow 6 hrs 50 mins
Total Distance 14.2 miles
Start G.R. 445802

A sign C.FP. BS3 near the toilet block on the campsite points to the cliffs. Follow this to the cliff top, then turn right on a grass path with excellent views over the rolling downs, towards Freshwater Bay (Plate 4). The cliffs along this section are subject to erosion, so take care. You may see Old Harry Rocks in the far distance on the mainland.

Arriving at Grange Farm Campsite, there is a chine, which you walk down and up the other side. The path skirts the outer perimeter of the site. Go through a small kissing gate out of the campsite to the cliff top again. Pass the row of holiday chalets just beyond the campsite and you arrive at a large white building, which is the Isle of Wight Pearl. Follow the C.FP. sign taking you inland onto the road and around to the other side of the Isle of Wight Pearl onto the cliff top again.

Continue on the cliff top path towards Freshwater Bay. Go over a stile, which brings you to Brook Green. Walk in front of the cottages to the road then divert back again onto the cliff path. This slight detour takes you around Brook Chine. Go through a kissing gate, a sign C.FP. BS98 states Freshwater Bay 3miles. The route along the cliff top is a good grass path. Pass through another kissing gate with views of Freshwater Bay ahead.

On reaching Compton Bay car park, walk through and cross another stile where your path ahead can be seen ascending over the hillside then down into Freshwater Bay. The good grass path takes you to the road but keep by the cliffs a little further before ascending some steps to emerge onto the road. Turn left and walk up and over the hill on the chalk path at the side of the road.

Descend on 1 of 3 chalk paths into Freshwater Bay (Plate 5). Just before your arrival you should pass a small monument erected in memory of a child who fell over the cliffs in 1846. The path finally descends some steps onto the promenade; this is a pleasant refreshment stop.

Walk along the side of the Albion Tavern to a bus shelter 100m further up on the left. A sign C.FP. F50 points left, this takes you along a narrow metalled road behind the shops. Looking ahead you will see your path ascending through 2 openings in the fences, leading to Tennyson Down. This is the most spectacular section of the walk.

The path ascending Tennyson Down starts with a good stone path, turning into a wide expanse of grass with gorse bushes in parts further on. Walk up and over the down, passing a Celtic cross in memory of Tennyson. Previously there had been a beacon here but it was removed in 1897 when Tennyson's monument was erected. The views in every direction are outstanding.

Take the long descent towards the Needles now before going over a stile on the final short ascent over West High Down, a sign states 1¼ miles to the Needles. Follow the path to the left of the coastguard cottages to a gate and stile. Go over the stile and on towards the new coastguard lookout station on the cliffs.

At the lower end of the coastguard cottages a C.FP. sign points to Alum Bay. Follow this on a chalk path running parallel with the road descending for 900m before you bear left to Alum Bay. Walk through Alum Bay car park passing the glass shop on your right and visitor attractions on the left. It was from near here that Marconi experimented with transmitting to ships at sea. Turn right at the roundabout and walk along the 2 way metalled road for 200m to a sign C.FP. T7 then turn left here by the entrance to Alum Bay tearooms.

Plate 5
Descending to Freshwater Bay on the chalk path.

21

Plate 6
Walking on Tennyson Down towards the Needles.

Walk up a narrow lane for 150m to another C.FP. sign to Totland and Colwell. Bear right here on an obvious path, which twists and turns as you ascend Headon Warren towards Headon Hill summit, passing a large Bronze Age burial mound off to your left. Pick up a gravel path on your right taking you over the summit. This path is winding as it descends and becomes narrower passing through heather and gorse. Bear left just beyond the summit onto a grass path towards Totland Bay.

You eventually walk along the side of Warren Cottage in the direction of Widdick Chine. Walk down the gravel track in front of Warren Cottage to the metalled road 150m further on. Turn left at the road and descend through the housing estate to a sign P.F. T33 Esplanade Walk. Follow this to Widdick Chine descending some steps to the promenade.

Turn right at the promenade passing Totland Bay old lifeboat house and the small pier. Continue on the promenade to Colwell Chine, which is 900m from the small pier just past Warden Point. There are numerous refreshment and sweet shops at Colwell Chine.

Should you be returning to your base after completing this section then walk up the road 500m from Colwell Chine to a bus stop on the A3054.

SECTION 4
Colwell Bay to Great Thorness (Holiday Park)
Time to Allow 7½ hrs
Total Distance 14.9 miles
Start G.R. 327879

Walk up from Colwell Chine passing refreshment kiosks and small shops to join the main A3054 road 500m on. You arrive at Colwell Bay Inn where you turn left. Walk up the road to a sign C.FP. F10 to your left, this is a metalled road passing Brambles Farm. The road now becomes a track where a sign C.FP. F9 Fort Victoria Country Park points up a narrow leafy lane. You emerge in Brambles Holiday Centre and a sign points to the right leading out onto a metalled road on a slight ascent. Walk to Monks Lane, then turn left.

Follow the C.FP. F6 sign along a metalled road for 200m passing a long row of new holiday chalets. The narrow path goes along by the side of a fence then skirts around private land before arriving at Cliff End Battery.

Follow the C.FP. on a pleasant walk through the woods. A sign states 'Welcome to Fort Victoria Country Park'. There are good views across the Solent. As you enter the park there are some seats and nearby some stone steps. The path is well defined going through the park. Keep on the main path unless you want to visit Fort Victoria Country Park, which is off to your left. Emerging onto a road, walk for a short distance to the first bend then bear left through the woods finally arriving on the promenade. Turn right walking towards Yarmouth, which can be seen ahead (Plate 7). Walk to the end of the promenade then onto a shale path, which leads to the main road.

Turn left and walk across the bridge over the River Yar into Yarmouth. Here there is an interesting harbour, pier and castle, which was built by Henry 8th as a sea defence, and is a popular refreshment stop.

Plate 7
Walking along the Promenade near Fort Victoria Country Park towards Yarmouth.

Plate 8
Wootton Bridge.

Coming off the bridge go straight across along Bridge Road past the church on your right. Turn left then first right beside Hardwoods shop then along the High Street leading out of town. You come to a grassed area on your left 350m further on, a sign C.FP Y11A points left onto the promenade. Walk along the promenade to another sign pointing back to the road, where you turn left and pass some houses on your right. At a bend a sign points to a P.F, ignore this and continue further along to a slight left hand bend to a sign C.FP.S43.

Turn left onto a wide pebbled road leading to the edge of the Solent. At the end of this unadopted road take the narrow path, which ascends through the woods for 1800m emerging near the Solent again. The path then leads away from the Solent up towards West Hamstead Farm. At a gap in the forest follow C.FP. sign on a distinctive path where as you walk towards the end of the forest there is a fork in the path. Take the right fork ascending to the end of the forest to a sign C.FP. S1. Continue in this direction to a small yellow arrow pointing to a grass field then another arrow pointing towards a section of forest passing a large white house on left.

Cross a stile where a sign C.FP. S1 is nearby. You will see some houses on the left and a gravel track but take a right hand path C.FP. S1. You come to another track and sign C.FP. S1 to the left, follow this to a sign on Sea View Road stating no unauthorised vehicles allowed. Continue ahead on a slight ascent along a straight road. Just before the brow of the hill follow a sign to the right through a 5-bar gate to a stile at the side of the field. Go over then over another stile into a field beside West Hampstead Farm. Walk along the side of the field then in front of the farm. Cross the access road to it then bear left on a grass field.

Proceed to a stile on the right at the bottom end of this field. Cross it and walk to the far end of the next field in the direction of Hampstead. Cross another stile onto a lane.

At a C.FP. S3 sign bear left then immediately right and follow the track round a left hand bend to Hampstead Farm. This path is just for walkers. Continue along side the farm buildings to the cottages where a sign points left on the C.FP. taking you on a good track down to the sea towards Hampstead Point. This is a pleasant walk with good views of the Solent ahead.

The track turns right at the beach and runs along the edge for a short distance passing a small memorial on your right. Turn right at a C.FP. sign S3 to Shalfleet, leading away from the beach. Continue on this obvious narrow path over some wooden bridges spanning the tidal areas then over a stile leading diagonally over a large field. To the left are views of Newtown River.

Cross another stile following a path along the edge of a field with the river on your left. At another stile and bridge follow the path in a square. This area is a tidal estuary. Follow the path, crossing over 2 stiles to a C.FP. sign S3 to Shalfleet 2½ miles. Turn right here and go up the long straight track passing Lower Hampstead Farm on the right. Pass Creek Farm cottage on the left and continue on this well defined track through a large wood.

Continue to a cross roads in the wood and a sign C.FP. S27, S11. Turn left here then over a bridge spanning the estuary. Once over the bridge turn left following the sign for a short distance through the wood. Go over another small bridge, take the path ahead and not the one on the right. This winds around the field emerging onto the A3054 road at the top of the field.

Turn left towards Shalfleet and walk to the New Inn at the traffic lights. Turn left here on the metalled road and just past the car park bear right on Mill Road. At Shalfleet Mill take the narrow track over a wooden bridge at the side of a house. Cross the stream then ascend a narrow track through a small wood emerging onto a metalled road.

Follow this road bearing left near Corf Farm onto a 'B' road. At a triangular piece of grass turn left passing a sign for Corf Scout Camp and continue on the road to a junction, signposted Newtown. Turn left here walking along Town Lane past Fleetlands Farm on the left. Continue over a small bridge ascending the metalled road towards Newtown.

You pass an old town hall on the right, dating back to 1699, now owned by the National Trust, then a house, turning right just after it. A sign states 'National Trust Newtown Nature Reserve'. Another sign near a kissing gate states P.F. Walk on the grass track over 9 fields and cross 2 stiles, go through a wood then over another stile onto a road.

Turn right on the C.FP. towards Windgate Copse. Follow this road along the edge of the forest to a junction 1600m further on. There is a new bungalow in front of you. At the junction turn left descending towards Porchfield area and Locks Farm.

Arriving at a cross roads with a small monument and a pub nearby, continue on the road to a small wood on the right. A sign states P.F. CB12A Thorness Bay and Gurnard. Turn left here, go over a stile then walk along the side of the wood then several fields towards South Thorness Farm crossing 2 stiles.

Walk along the side of the field then follow a yellow arrow right to go around the farm buildings. Go over a stile onto a metalled road. Should you be camping here then turn left and walk out of the village of Great Thorness following the concrete road to the campsite 450m further on. Alternatively should you intend to return to your base then turn right after crossing the stile and walk for 600m to a 'B' road then turn right again at a junction and walk for 3200m to the main A3054 road to connect with a bus back to base.

SECTION 5
Great Thorness (Holiday Park) to Ryde
Time to Allow 7 hrs
Total Distance 12.5 miles
Start G.R. 451926

Leaving South Thorness Farm turn left, pass some old chalets on your right and look for a C.FP. sign CB24 nearby. Follow the sign crossing a stile into a field. Cross a further 2 stiles in front then turn right between a short avenue of trees to a C.FP. sign. Turn left here walking down a metalled road through a large caravan park, bearing left at the camp shop then right walking towards the wood and beach beyond. There are openings between the hedge at the lower right side of the site and a path across open grassland leads to a picnic area. Keep to the edge of the beach.

As you walk around the edge of Thorness Bay there is a small concrete bridge, which you cross, then go over a stile. Follow the cliff path around the headland over a narrow, undulating and uneven path. This short section is uninteresting with only occasional views across the Solent. The path eventually descends behind some holiday chalets and onto a metalled road.

Follow the descending road left, ignore the P.F. sign on the sea wall, instead follow the road round taking the first main road on the left. At the next bend ascend a hill through a housing estate; turn left descending to the sea. A sign C.FP. points left down a short lane to the promenade. This is known as Princes Esplanade. Follow the road around Egypt Point, the most northerly point on the island. Walk on the promenade into Cowes then along the main street by the shops and the ferry terminal.

Follow the signs leading along Medina Road to the floating bridge that takes you to East Cowes. This is a free foot passenger service. Just upstream from the floating bridge is Westland Aerospace, which builds hovercraft. At East Cowes, walk straight ahead, then at a fork in the road bear right onto York Avenue ascending a hill for 2900m on the A3021 passing a school halfway up.

Walking along York Avenue you will pass 2 entrances to Osborne House on your left then a school on your right. Cross here then turn left on Alverston Road beside Whippingham Community Association Hall situated on the corner. Walk to the end of Alverston Road then turn right heading towards Wootton Bridge.

Walk along Brocks Copse Road descending towards Brocks Copse, then ascend a street to a junction. Turn left, then immediately right along a street called Footways. This takes you through an estate to a junction with Church Road. A P.F. sign points down a narrow walkway behind some houses, then follow a C.FP. sign beside some garages. Walk around the garages and again behind some houses descending towards Wootton Bridge. Walk around some more garages then another path takes you behind the houses, to emerge at The Sloop Inn at Wootton Bridge (plate 8).

Cross the bridge and walk up the A3054 road passing a sign for Kite Hill Camping Park. At the brow of the hill where the road bears right, take a left turn on P.F. R1 on Ashlake Copse Lane walking down a narrow metalled road to some trees at the bottom. Continue on a straight path through the woods onto a gravel track. You come to a wider metalled road, carry straight on to a sign C.FP. R1 Fishbourne Lane.

Walk up this narrow lane to a road. Turn left onto the B3331 passing the Fishbourne Ferry Terminal. Just beyond is the Fishbourne Inn. Turn right on the Public Bridleway R3 opposite the pub onto a track between the hedges. At the top go through a gate passing the entrance to Quarr Abbey, then down Quarr Road passing the old abbey ruins. Henry 8th dissolved the abbey in 1537. Walk up the shale path to a sign stating C.FP. R45 Church Road. Turn left here onto a road, follow it round to the church; do not follow the sign to Binstead.

Turn right in front of the church and walk towards a green sign R48 Ryde town centre. Descend and cross a stream keeping the golf course to your right, then up Ladies Walk to the corner of the A3054 road. Turn left here following a C.FP. R94 sign Ryde ¾mile on a wide gravel track then onto Spencer Road. Walk through the housing estate to a sign on the right pointing down Buckingham Road towards Ryde Pier. Walk down bearing right onto St. Thomas Street, along a tree lined lane onto a wider street, then turn left past a car park emerging at the bottom of the hill near Ryde roundabout and the pier.

You have now completed the 70mile Isle of Wight Coastal Footpath - CONGRATULATIONS!

Tourist Information Centres

Ryde -	Western Esplanade	01983 562905
Sandown -	8 High Street	01983 403886
Shanklin -	67 High Street	01983 862942
Ventnor -	34 High Street	01983 853625
Yarmouth -	The Quay	01983 760015
Cowes -	Fountain Quay	01983 291914
Newport -	High Street	01983 823366
Island Bus Information -		01983 532373
Tourist Information Website -		www.islandbreaks.co.uk

The map required for your journey is:-
  Ordnance Survey - Outdoor Leisure No.29
  Isle of Wight 1:25000 scale

Mileage between prominent landmarks on the coastal path calculated to include ascents and descents.

	Km	Miles
Ryde Pier to Seaview	5.1	3.1
Seaview to Sandown	13.7	8.5
Sandown to Ventor	9.1	5.6
Ventor to Niton	7.3	4.5
Niton to Atherfield (Chine Farm Campsite)	9.2	5.7
Atherfield to Freshwater Bay	12.9	8.0
Freshwater Bay to The Needles	4.9	3.1
The Needles to Colwell	5.0	3.1
Colwell to Yarmouth	5.1	3.2
Yarmouth to Shalfleet	11.8	7.3
Shalfleet to Great Thorness	7.1	4.4
Great Thorness to Cowes Floating Bridge	8.0	5.0
Cowes Floating Bridge to Wootton Bridge	6.4	4.0
Wootton Bridge to Ryde Pier	5.7	3.5
	111.3	69.2

Walking times between prominent landmarks.

Section 1

	Hrs	Mins
Ryde Pier to Nettlestone Point		50
Nettlestone Point to Nodes Point Hol. Park	1	05
Nodes Point Hol. Park to Bembridge Lifeboat Stat.	1	05
B'bridge Lifeboat Stat. to Culver Down Monument	1	20
Culver Down Monument to Sandown	1	10
Sandown to Hope Beach-Shanklin Camping		45
	6	15

Section 2

	Hrs	Mins
Hope Beach to Ventnor	2	00
Ventnor to Niton	2	35
Niton to Chale Church	1	10
Chale Church to Atherfield-Chine Farm Camping	1	40
	7	25

Section 3

	Hrs	Mins
Atherfield Campsite to Isle of Wight Pearl	1	15
Isle of Wight Pearl to Freshwater Bay	2	35
Freshwater Bay to The Needles	1	10
The Needles to Colwell Bay-Freshwater camping		50
	5	50

Section 4

Colwell Bay to Yarmouth	1	40
Yarmouth to Gt. Thorness-Hol.Park	4	50
	6	30

Section 5

Gt. Thorness to Cowes Floating Bridge	2	25
Cowes Floating Bridge to Wootton Bridge	1	55
Wootton Bridge to Ryde Pier	1	40
	6	00

Total Walking Time 32 Hours

The times given above are based on average walking times. Allowances should be made for fitness, weather conditions, amount of equipment/weight of rucksack being carried and the number of people walking.

The sections have been divided to enable those walking the full route to stop at the campsites shown whilst still having time each day to enjoy the attractions and amenities on route.

Attractions on the Coastal Footpath Route

1. Ryde - Ice Rink, Ten Pin Bowling, Golf, Swimming Pool
2. Seaview - Flamingo Park
3. Bembridge - Shipwreck Centre
4. Sandown - Isle of Wight Zoo, Golf, Swimming Pool
5. Shanklin - Chine
6. Ventnor - Botanical Gardens, Rare Breeds Park, Smuggling Museum
7. St. Catherine's Point - Lighthouse
8. Chale - Blackgang Chine
9. Brightstone - Dinosaur Farm
10. Chilton Chine - Isle of Wight Pearl
11. The Needles - Old Battery, Needles Viewpoint
12. Alum Bay - Needles Pleasure Park (chair lift)
13. Yarmouth - Fort Victoria Country Park, Harbour
14. Cowes - Model Railway
15. East Cowes - Osborne House

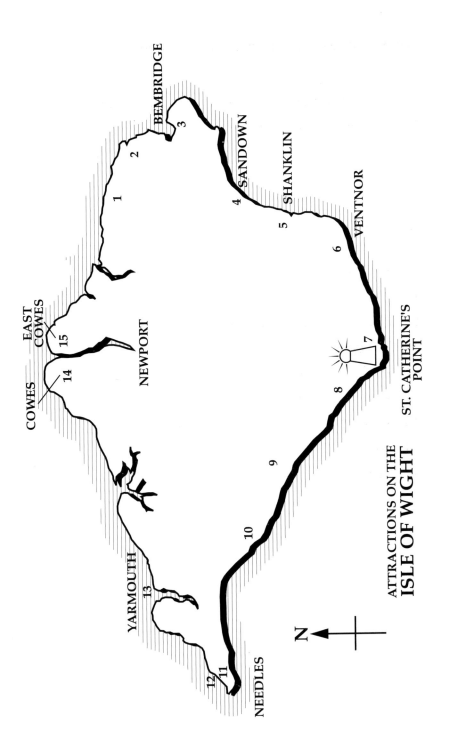

ATTRACTIONS ON THE
ISLE OF WIGHT

BEMBRIDGE

SANDOWN

SHANKLIN

VENTNOR

ST. CATHERINE'S
POINT

NEWPORT

EAST
COWES

COWES

YARMOUTH

NEEDLES

N

Campsites on Route

* Rating

1. Seaview - Pondwell Camping Holidays 01983 612330   3
2. Nodes Point - Holiday Park   01983 872401   3
3. Bembridge - Whitecliff Bay Holiday Park 01983 872671   4
4. Lower Hyde (Shanklin) - Holiday Village 01983 866131   4
5. Atherfield - Chine Farm Campsite   01983 740228   2
6. Brightstone Bay - Grange Farm Campsite 01983 740296   3
7. Brook - Compton Farm   01983 740215   2
8. Totland - Stoats Farm Camping   01983 755258   2
9. Freshwater - Heathfield Farm Campsite 01983 756756   3
10. Cowes - Thorness Bay Holiday Park   01983 523109   3
11. East Cowes - Waverley Park Holiday Centre 01983 293452   2
12. Wootton Bridge - Kite Hill Farm   01983 882543   4

Book in advance especially during busy holiday times.

Bed & Breakfast accommodation hotline: - 01983 813813

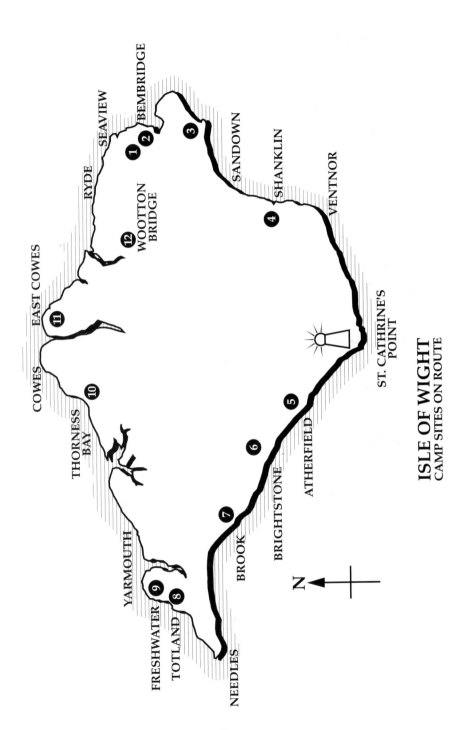

ISLE OF WIGHT
CAMP SITES ON ROUTE

BEMBRIDGE

SEAVIEW

RYDE

SANDOWN

WOOTTON
BRIDGE

SHANKLIN

VENTNOR

EAST COWES

COWES

ST. CATHRINE'S
POINT

THORNESS
BAY

ATHERFIELD

BRIGHTSTONE

BROOK

YARMOUTH

FRESHWATER

TOTLAND

NEEDLES

N

40

Public Houses on Route

Ryde - Fowlers
Nettlestone Point - Battery Inn, Old Fort Inn
Bembridge - Pilot Boat Inn
East Bembridge - Crab & Lobster
Whitecliff Bay - Nab Bars
Culver Down - The Culvar Haven Inn
Sandown - Jolly Sailor
Appley Steps, Luccombe - Fishermans Cottage
Ventnor - Landsdowne Pub, The Bell, The Mill Bay,
         The Spy Glass Inn
Blackgang Chine - The Old Coach House
Chale -Wight Mouse Inn
Freshwater Bay - Albion Tavern
Totland Bay - The Waterfront
Colwell - The Colwell Bay Inn
Yarmouth - The Kings Head, Wheatsheaf Inn,
           The Bugle Inn, The George Hotel
Shalfleet - The New Inn, The Sportsmans Rest
Gurnard Bay - Salty Seadog, The Woodvale
Cowes - Harbour Lights, The Three Crowns,
        Fountain Hotel, Vectis Tavern, Pier View,
        Anchor Inn, Painter Arms, Duke of York
East Cowes - Prince of Wales
Wootton Bridge - The Sloop Inn
Fishbourne - Fishbourne Inn

One particular café worth mentioning is the Octopus'
Garden in Cowes for it's unusual decor and theme.

Post Walk

Have you enjoyed this walk? Have you found it a challenge? If so then consider walking The Isle of Wight North to South - East to West. These walks have fabulous views and good scenery from start to finish.

The book has two walks of 18 and 28 miles across the centre of the island from Cowes to St Catherine's lighthouse and Bembridge to The Needles. Both walks are divided in two so you can conveniently walk half of one route and still have time to visit attractions during the day. Each route can be comfortably completed in two days.

The author has produced a number of other guides covering walks and challenges throughout Great Britain. These are shown at the front of this book or you can visit Challenge Publications website.

All books are available from most bookshops by quoting the ISBN No. if not in stock. Alternatively they are available direct from

Challenge Publications
7 Earlsmere Drive
Barnsley
S71 5HH

Visit our website and view each title: -
www.chall-pub.fsnet.co.uk

Will you accept the Challenge?

NOTES